AMONG THE STATUES THERE

Among the Statues There

A collection of poems
by
AUSTIN C. MORGAN

Adelaide Books
New York / Lisbon
2020

AMONG THE STATUES THERE
A collection of poems
By Austin C. Morgan

Copyright © by Austin C. Morgan
Cover design © 2020 Adelaide Books

Published by Adelaide Books, New York / Lisbon
adelaidebooks.org

Editor-in-Chief
Stevan V. Nikolic

All rights reserved. No part of this book may be reproduced in any manner whatsoever without written permission from the author except in the case of brief quotations embodied in critical articles and reviews.

For any information, please address Adelaide Books
at info@adelaidebooks.org
or write to:
Adelaide Books
244 Fifth Ave. Suite D27
New York, NY, 10001

ISBN: 978-1-952570-67-4

Printed in the United States of America

For M, D, Delaney, & Cecilia

Contents

Foreword to *Among the Statues There* **9**

PART I **13**

    Among the Statues There **15**

    The Doctor's Daughter **47**

    In Lot of a Station Nightly **51**

    Agartha **53**

PART II **71**

    Portrait of a Late-August Evening **73**

    Recollections of Bathing Street at Night **75**

    High Moon in July **77**

    Eastertime Blues **79**

    The Witchcat **81**

    Sketches from *The City & the Sea* **83**

    Song of Two Lovers Glimpsed from Afar **91**

    On Love **93**

About the Author **95**

Foreword to Among the Statues There

by Kurt Cassidy-Gabhart

There is little doubt that in recent decades transgressions have been committed against the world of art. Creative decisions are being executed in deference to pecuniary considerations. The pawns of these machinations are not artists but profiteers; their Machiavellian insensibility has succeeded the grace of the poets. Art ought to be viewed as a sort of pronouncement, a validation of the voice of the poor, in a government and justice system in which profit alone determines truth. If art becomes void through profit, so too does the recognition of the less fortunate: capital once again confirms its primacy over everything.

The world needs artists like Mr. Morgan. He is a poet who respects the form, and the historical authority that established it. He does not, like the majority of modern artists (or more properly doomed aspirants), denigrate the wisdom of the

Greats; but he reveres it, in that it guides him to innovate upon the form often led astray by capital.

That art is a sort of subjective term to which no definitive elaboration can be attested posits the ignorance of the modern individual, as well as his blind irreverence toward authority. "Art is a capacity to create," said Aristotle, "involving a true course of reasoning." Kant expanded this definition many years later, in that it only arises from a "talent for producing that for which no definite rule can be given," although there is a basic rule which may be "gathered from the performance, i.e., from the product, which others may use to put their own talent to the test." It is because of the wanton deprecation of such aestheticism that art suffered direly. The modern individual, unamenable to discipline, revels in his blindness.

The decline of religious influence has incurred ambiguity in the objective of art. What was once quite clearly the representation of things divine or otherworldly has now become what proves to be the least expense and the greatest convenience. Capital, now, is patron: the objective is profit. This substitution is formidable, for genuine works of poetry, such as the present, of music and painting, are means of teaching us about ourselves and the world around us. An understanding of the interdependency of everything elicits our empathy, and this understanding can only be attained through genuine works of art.

This collection may not be that in which one fell swoop revives the dwindling significance of art, but it certainly does stand as a testament of its revitalization. It lends aid to the fundamental effort of a Neo-Renaissance, to which Mr.

AMONG THE STATUES THERE

Morgan is doubtlessly an adherent, and proclaims in unwavering terms that in a time of odious morbidity, art is our one salvation.

K.C.G.

August 2019

Kurt Cassidy-Gabhart is an author and filmmaker based in Jasper, Indiana.

PART I

In the calm moonlight, so lovely fair
That makes the birds dream in the slender trees,
While fountains dream among the statues there;
Slim fountains dream in silver ecstasies
 — Paul Verlaine, "Clair de Lune"
 (Faulkner translation)

Come about hard and join
The young and often spring you gave
 — Van Dyke Parks & Brian Wilson,
 "Surf's Up"

AMONG THE STATUES THERE

I

Beware!
Winter's noxious glow,
fallen against evening's
 windowpane
as autumn shall freeze
& the Capricorn
 hour
melts unto
 Spring.

I'd lived alone in those years —
 emerald draped delicately
 across the sobbing napes of
 our muses there,
curtains billowing by
 candleglow,

warm mist of May crept
 softly 'neath my resting
doorframe
 & I would dream of where
I would find you upon
 the stair
 — begotten &
 beheld —
 still dreaming of cogs turning

  within
  your Eastertide machine
"& dressed in white, just as the bone
  'neath the surface of my
   paper moon

& within my virgin's
 Spring,
I shall carry your name behind
        truthful lips —
 closest thing
I may know to holding you
     so

summer nights
 so far from this room
summertime
 by light of August moon,
you fan the flame within my soul
  it burns from
 this day forth
& if you must slumber
perhaps I shall be found there
 in dreaming

II

That night from afar,
I watched her face,
pale as porcelain

AMONG THE STATUES THERE

    moonlight,
fallen across the belly
    of their gloaming:
such secrets, this low vigil – saudade –
secret streets, silent water — saudade —
    whispered across her rostrum of light.
The sound crept softly to me,
low & lovely as the scent
    of melting snow in February,
& how I dreamt I would gaze upon
such a face, in its
silent hint of
    displeasure, at which
the fruit within her cheeks
    would swell, cascading shadow
caressing hand as black as night,
    or should I stand to witness such joy
    in crossing your Archimedean features,
that the spirits of the auditorium may drift
    lightly for to nestle within the
hollow of said cheek —
            saudade
                saudade.

III

O strangest games
& velvet rings,
I watch you sink
from a streetcar beyond —

Austin C. Morgan

Blossoms bloom cherry
    atop the ruinous springhouse,
its children glow by light of
      candlestick moon,
     lanterns within the fog rolling
    in rhythm to the swilling of strings
        swollen, too —
Diana, Mars,
        brought together,
those strings, they sing
    for me
in symphonic sorrow, as willows will rustle
          before the iron gate &
crystallization will salt all hearts
              thereafter.
    You trace the bow,
fingertips which grace the neck,
such music heard by none
       but I & night
          behind her curtain
                sighs,
while against the crowd
seraphim swans,
scarlet-haired,
loom high behind her to
whisper "even feeble dreamers long
              to know
                      the
                            morning"

AMONG THE STATUES THERE

IV

Shallot shall be
   my one true love — adrift
toward the isles of Camelot,
   weeping in wait,
             lonesome, beguiled,
however, I am no longer so
          Arthurian,
asleep in pollen grass of
             May,
soul wound as the wooded path
where virginal magnolias bloom
          painted, ever so
            into the canvas stretch.

O how weary I have grown
of foreign currencies
upon the board before me
& dining, ever-presently,
among my own company
while the barmaid with a face of
   Roman tragedy
eludes me,
        flutters past,
               evermore.

In the park, by the moonlight,
painters & poets
   line the way

& I've waited with a kiss
    textured poppyseed upon tongue
for to pass through her
              Christian curtain
& fall against her
                lily lip —
   subtle smile (a mystery) of
   Mona Lisa with strings
(ave),
ruby mouth in Miranda,
spilling such a lovely
      sonnet-dusk,
as I found myself lost at
the core of her
      nocturne,
         lost & lovely – ave.

Should one perceive
these words upon the stone,
forever I shall take
she who has beheld
strangest scent of my
nestled-silhouette roses,
      ave
        ave, no longer

& at behest of my
lowly lunar spirits,
I haunt the glass &
the beautiful still
                dance.

AMONG THE STATUES THERE

My sister weeps
   beside the Roman statues,
since fallen to vine
        & decay.
My sister weeps
    — lunette glow —
she weeps,
   although
              I no longer hear the sound of her voice.

V

O great pillars,
   crashing Luna!
Standing bare behind
            her great risen door
            (great wooden faces),
present to me   church floors
            great doors
            crimson as the tam she
            wore upon the halo of her
                hair; backward glance
                through the falling snow,
                a blackened strand to dance
                across her forehead
& how these cold cemetery eves
are of such essence to me —
            mausoleum streets wind forth
            unto soft martyrdom atop turpentine
            Xibalba — place of fear shall never

    rest & founding humor in all but I,
    overshadowed by handsome friends
   & ghosts with twilit eyes,
& how my own have searched for you — sea with no horizon.
 Wander midnight silk beyond restriction within these walls

& how I am mad!
how I am wrong
to have cradled you
so closely
 inside my mind,
blemishes unbeknownst to this room
   & history,
   sweet history,
   behind your eyes.
 I fold pale
  wing,
for to press my hand against
 my chest as my mother ponders
       "boundaries" to appease
these ungrateful strangers.
Who are they, seated before her,
within my home
home of
liberty
& of persuasion toward
 failure?
Such foolishness here
   tonight!

AMONG THE STATUES THERE

Might I be found there,
or perhaps merely ebb &
                    flow? I shall abide —
  worn, awakened,
      blankets across their slumbering faces

& I emerge anew!
   Borne by sheeted morn',
  into the light
her chiffon streets
  are vessels   so far
      behind, alas,
  I shall recall,
  I shall recall,

while upon my return, my dreams shall be
of gardens grown & painted Venetian
   faces in the crowd near Mecca,
carrying forth an air of orchids blooming
     scarlet   & crowded cobblestones down
anemic alleyways breathe
   beneath ancient milieu,
lined by golden streetlamp,
   ascent high beyond that of
        thine angels
   & as had Wilde, I shall swoon —
even beg of her to sing to me
her later tales of the afterworld,
told only by flicker of resting
                iris,
            this strange, unruly twilight.

Caught between these globes (ancient)
   & into the water below,
stranger lives lurk beneath;
          never seek the call
               down there.

I shall pause among the galleries
& dream of meeting her
at the back of the Store,
should I return to confide in her
this vast affection
   & inherent desire dreamt
          down winter streets —
   her divine & charitable song.

Peculiar & charmed,
I've longed to find here
among the
         Rembrandts, where
      Paxton's pearls gleam golden upon
         the naked torso of another finely threaded muse
                      within hue of
                Richardson, her boney
              Streetglow,
        where I am captivated by recollection
of strolling forlorn round the
   public Square,
where lecherous streetsides are luminous by
ectoplasmic lantern light
& did I dream I saw you in the tall window

AMONG THE STATUES THERE

some looming loft?
Lost spec, thicker rim,
with lips pursed as though
that gracious audience had thrown
    roses,
        roses,
            roses upon her stage
& there I shall witness her arrival,
awaiting the twenty-third as if the
            Second Coming & what of the terminology
                      — saudade —
I dare not speak it, though,
as well as her name,
I dare not speak it so.

VI

Tonight,
among the misty groves,
milk of the moon
glistens upon her skin
& I've waited for this
among the drifting apple blossoms,
my steely soul
    eternally bent,
yet to no avail
    have such hopes arrived.

Fairest undertone:
light of blue

swells in swirling hue, flaming chivalry
as the centuries dance & drift away
across the cradle of your face,
      pristine —

beside a frozen lake,
(partial), pale
ice gathered like glass shattered
      round the rim,
 faint lunation above
hangs as though haunted — transparent —
 & should she know my name,
as I do swoon for to recall
such honest
 memory
crashing through
 nighttime air,
thin &
 misrepresented —

(still same) Sun is of better hours,
but it is cooler in the forest —
million winding pathways
from which I might not
 return.

Lake — Patoka —
 blue-river underbelly,
 face of dawn,
beachside, I have roamed.

AMONG THE STATUES THERE

There is a spirit which glides
    beside you,
he is conventional
        convoluted
          & alizarin,
        waiting there despite her roses
        with petals folded by midnight.

On this day: "God Has Healed,"
Hebrew, I embed her name
within the sound of my voice.
Lymantria dispar dispar,
flutters against the leaves
& Trouvelot had waned his soul,
children beneath floral luna,
petals drift as embers
in garden-glow, eternal June –
                (expelled from the Store,
            like Pound unto
              Rome…
          not to keep, not to want
            & never to return) –

I see hazy, blissful glory,
as I bask within your rays.
Stronger, not,
beaten, feathers
scatter airborne in flight
to their way along

Infinite autumnal fire,
juniper hums by April,
unfolded for to bear witness
to this deep & vacant pool
   of yearning.
Sky, a crumbled sienna, & tufts of grey
                              Beyond,
as the fog creeps, once more,
across the water — glass —
deep as echoes through cavernous
                       history.
Weeping softly hidden behind Mayan curtain,
such stunning animals waltz
across the textile
& in such, you are clad;
softly creatures coo,
sounds of love having been
                  made
from upon your marble disposition,
like a muse lost behind
   plate-mirror, this display
I have come to see,
long to see,
   forevermore,
for I've not known
the taste of your lips,
   the distance of your moon.
Must I hunger here
before the Idols,
adorned in finer thread &
   wreaths of olive?

AMONG THE STATUES THERE

Here I linger.
faced lonesome by
   the hours
        (upon each, a fading star)
with my burgundy heart.
Strange portmanteaus,
secrets read aloud
from lips pursed & kept
as you knelt before the children,
hair-hued harvested erosion,
cascading down your face.

O how I long to be so young
upon the wall
      beside her,
which looms between
the city & the sea —
how I long to be so young
              eternally!

VII

The lovers,
   rendered wan,
lips cool & pale
   as glistening treetop frost;
my right eye shall see
              beyond
the hills, the Sun,

while my left shall be
given over   to blindness,
& I still read her name
   written there in the
                Store.

VIII

Our voices dissipate
against the orchestral
   backdrop
of your lonesome, lovely,
   wedding-tune.
Painted crowds bow
   by nighttime
& the villagers dance onward,
for my longing is to last
till light of
        Dawn,
where my essence has been
                freed from
her cheeks,
   carved & high
(as ivory shall be) —
endless passage of August,
with hair wound tightly round
boughs of holly, pristine
pining, eternally
poised, artful

AMONG THE STATUES THERE

& gently, we shall be
   betrayed
within a glare of
distaste projected upon
another lover's silver verse
& I dream
ashamedly,
I drown
alone.

Sugar lagoon,
   such pleasantries:
Selene submerged
   so far beneath,
her idolatrous figurines
line the floor —
marble & Rome
dance upon the altar,
haunting drowned cotillion
& ivory archways
(amethyst),
each roaming afterthought
of her voice,
its strange inflection
carries onward like
   whispers through moonlit boughs —
o jealous sea!
   I have fallen
        before thee

in hope of reprieve
from those chords enchanted, played
                    that lone night as
                    the violet hour fell to ruin
& all classicism drained
    from her face in the light
until the vines of pastoral ivy
    unraveled from her hair
                    like dust.

My love has been but a dream
& no ink does clot beneath my flesh —
I may never know such a golden way again.

"Somehow, I've not known you,"
    declaration rung through rusted gates
tumbling forth from on high,
    this expatriate chorus
        tells no lies
as the Piper (contemporarily chic
    with his barroom sensibilities)
casting a layer of shade across her
                    darkest eye
& the heart,
once beaten,
shatters in rhythm
to the Devastator's hollow tune,
which stole me,
    like a fool,
        away from her.

IX

Azure is Heaven,
   which weeps down
         from above.
Such homely   faces,
ill & impoverished
      — bitter —
tempestuous throughout the dust
              & ruins, to gaze
               upon thee in
                 hatred, as in
                   love —
they have been my brothers,
   by law of Adam,
spoken near a
      fencepost in Eden
         (an ancestry of Hermetic
             ministry
     torn to ribbons & tangled as
          this congregation,
                cradled softly by
        dreamless
         Gomorrah).
  Azure is Heaven
    (being the final
      kingdom within reach),
resting wearily among the
       olive branches.

Austin C. Morgan

The youth sit proudly
   upon dusk's pavilion,
once sung in her name.
   This tree, devoid of leaf,
shivering naked,
       silent
against the planetary glow
   of another eternal tomorrow,
      …who are we?

   Like pale glow trickling
through evening-blind,
   comrades underestimate me,
despite all that I have given —
       passion,
          the hours,
          all that I have given.

   & the Piper fell asleep
among futile Spanish roses,
   but the muse has chosen
to remain there beside him.
   Marigolds,
      wilted,
           by strange light
   detergent breeze
     on March evenings,
never known

AMONG THE STATUES THERE

        (& when the rain roars
        against the windowpane,
          my mother sighs,
          to rest within
        her American eyes,
          & the dreams
       upon the doorframe,
           evermore
           evermore,

          my mother sighs,
         for to rest within
        her American eyes)

But what of the kingdom I have built?
    I shall roam its noctambulant hallways
with a streak of subtle
        vanity
  painted across my chest
& I ask "will you ever know
& will it be of any concern to you,
this kingdom I have built —
be it love — this kingdom?"

      Have I dreamt this world before?
      "turn away then,
            let him suffer."

Yellow fields embody hues
    of paler-flickered lanternlight
aglow, through the fields roam
    peasants of bluer earth,
removing thee from the pain
    of Southern stately dwelling:
                      my striking home of
                        terror
                      & chaos
                            masters lachrymose
                        & their raging hands
                            glow argent through
sunset,
                          arching, always,
                                through sunset.

X

Soliloquies of the Moon

MAIDEN
(as inspiration):
                Hark!
Every dream shall be madness,
    as I am the pistil of the universe,
with my hair tinted eventide,
    flowing grand didactic river evermore —
o sweet red wine,
    & my voice — choir of midnight!

AMONG THE STATUES THERE

I stand clad in evening gowns
     received
by the great
  Northern winds,
splendid royalty,
    my eyes etched
       upon canvas of gods
     gazing down upon thee.

My seraphim sisters,
      bathing in the ardent surf
of ancient reddened seas, which I
                      turn,
water warm & welcoming to thee
     spilling
        endlessly,
my seraphim sister,
   name unspoken,
      fallen,
born unto
babbling kings
   & their
      concubine ladies —
illness through the streets
spread wings of
  terror,
glanced upon her mother
      (solemn, youthful rage),
          to forsake her.

Revolt!
o how we were
so demure
  in our own graceful
      ways,
for ashamed
  was she
 to have borne this
    child,
high above,
 among the stars
& to dishonor,
  such fools,
our parents, clad in robes
 of luna & stellae
saw not the armies nearing –
 four hundred of them
graced with strength
 of four hundred tempests
     on wing,

while some millennia later,
  men would find our fragments:
stony limbs
  of my seraphim sister,
among the ruins of
  a banished temple,
laid to rest by
  bashful hands of the faithful,
communicants,

AMONG THE STATUES THERE

    shadows painted against walls
    of abandoned seaside cities. Red,
color of the sky upon Revelation

   — Art must surely be
                      this perpetual youth
calling from deep within
                      my soul —
lustful, arrogant
lovers run naked,
past a resting statuette, Pan:
    grinning,
        wreath upon his horns,
            & vapid, these lovers,
                frolic blossoms of virginity
            wound tritely upon their crowns.

Mission house alight,
   face painted with bells,
I gazed curiously
unto them in such great
                  folly
& gleamed down upon
   illuminating the ever-present
                      darkness —

such romance from afar,
never having known her touch.

This abstinent beauty,
drying in the palace of the Sun,
dancing upon the ruins of pleasure,
the dome of which had collapsed,
when the heart she bore
fell from grace unto another,
only to emerge, aflame,
from the crashing waves
of gallant sea,
                    the spirit of her heart's return:
              this is truly art.

the most genuine expression, intrinsic motion —

                            be it art.
                                ca. 1469/87

MOTHER
(as memory):
        Painted doves
        upon precious china,
        I am cast away from
        from the embrace,
        of my idolater children.
        thrones of ivory
        upon which they dwell,
        looming far above
        the atmosphere,

AMONG THE STATUES THERE

while I am partial
to that of Earth beneath me.

my age is that of weariness,
the future no longer so distant,
and the past having faded to a pale glimmer.
I, grand puppeteer,
guiding the sea in and out of slumber.
come forth, dear ones,
come and linger beside me.

waning,
lonesome,
air above Naples,
haunt the fishermen
gathered at its ports.
one wields a wooden lute,
or perhaps a century mandolin,
singing songs of his one love,
a sobbing figure on a foreign shore.

he sings of this love
and of his loss,
of meadows at twilight
and crowded streets in the rain,
soul no longer joyous,
the chime of his clock, midnight,
clothing rumpled and ragged.
those who gaze upon him

Austin C. Morgan

recall evenings of such warmth
& cheer
littered counters,
clinking glass,
nothing but time

who is she,
this lover of whom he sings?
how well does he recall
her spiral locks of coal,
her ghostly complexion
the way her dress
did billow against
the seaside wind, so far from here
her name, be it Sol
be it Esmerelda
who is she,
this woman of whom he sings?

now sailing ships have ceased
& the surface of the sea must rest,
but there she lingers, evermore,
within the hallway of his recollection.

is it she of whom he dreams
when he succumbs to sleep
in his otherwise empty bed?
it is she of whom he shall sing
when dusk has fallen

AMONG THE STATUES THERE

  and the men of the port
  gather 'round?
  her absence,
  this longing,
  a tune as sweet
  as the stars of Heaven
  where statues do weep
  & memory prevails — an endless sea
          ca. 1828/29

CRONE
(as mortality):
  — earth,
 brittle as bone,
  foxtails,
    mi culpa tastes
   like papaya seed, tastes like
    Death, for
 toward the waxing,
  bitter I have grown,
 such luck to have
  amidst the grand
     Seventeen;
 now I am lost to time
    (lilies upon the water),
 & Jupiter weighs
    heavily,
 a storm which refuses to
    cease,

fraudulent masculinity,
        those beneath
(persuasion toward battle, that is) mere echoes
           down the passage of history
    …and I fade
    this lore,
        grand mosaic

      of what love
          could have
             been
still it was beautiful,
it was divine
    I shall recall thee
        in perfect form,
    there upon the dais
    till my final breath
has passed,
    upon which my love
    shall
    be as in a
    dream,
        spoken in murmurs
            across lips awakened,
      acknowledged only by fools
    & dreamers, alike.

AMONG THE STATUES THERE

…but until the day has arrived,
        I will linger lonesome,
                forevermore,
within flux – infinite,
        passages of the great
               artesian
                    Hour.

                January 22nd — March 8, 2018

THE DOCTOR'S DAUGHTER
for A.

La Luna:
   of elegant pearl,
veiled by threadlike
   summercloud
— humid & surrounded
        by fleeting hue of
        communal festivity
           aglow,
streets slickened by silver
glimmer of mid-August rain.

across the cusp's dizzying lip,
its eventual zenith,
feathers of her wing
      ruffled as she
           found me there upon
           the courthouse stair
           & I greeted her with
                eyes wide aglow,
                burning,
                burning, whispered:

                alas, alas

pillars of eventide
shouldered the weight
of Heaven spread above,

Austin C. Morgan

the seraphim in struggle
to cease its aimless spilling
upon the congregants
           below

& I asked,   was it you who dwelt behind
            summer shutters of azure dreaming
            & among the copper statuettes
            of the Eastern ghost, which lingered
            just beyond the stairwell — royal oak?

& I pondered that
            banality; its contemporaneous association
                with love & all
                which stands
                      beyond & abloom,
                      with petals of an
                      endless sixteen —
            as was she —
                      derivative of such
                      pubescent knowledge
                      gleaned from
                      a nymph of the
                            Sea
        (mystery to me)

& I was pardoned,
I was absolved by her prayer:
Friday faith known to
so very few,
not unlike those
surrounding,

AMONG THE STATUES THERE

or that archaic Iranian upon
the mountain's peak.
He spoke of mortality within the veins of
twilight by desert's gleam,
but upon eager descent, found all eyes fixated
                upon earthly
                        travesty
                            (pitfall of better men)

while beneath many-an-

        illuminating-bulb, we spoke of
        verse
          & of kindly chariot
        hymnals unaware
            of the melody's winding halt
            — so, chimed the churchbell
            — so, clanged the eveningbell
        "midnight: cusp of nocturne,
        hour of palest fingertips"
                & that she
                would eventually
                part from
                    me

    — for she aspired for greater spirit
& in her hour of womanhood, departed for to walk
the crimson hillsides of
distant seaside cities,
leaving behind only stray feathers
within her wake,

Austin C. Morgan

as I witnessed petals of demise: faded sixteen,
all which remains, tome of her father.
my only isthmus, tome of her father.

how have I recalled   her eyes of woven
                                               silk

                             her mouth of timely
                                     riddle

                             her face in sculpted
                                   precision

                             & her soul to rest against
                                   the Olympian base, for
draw stranger envy from the souls of Creation
                                   (diviner)
                             as They gaze on;

shall I continue in this recollection by
                               her absence,
shall I rest against the Mount
                        & perhaps upon her swift
                             return
                 we might meet once more,
                             finished by those souls
                       ever-burnt

March 15th, 2018

IN LOT OF A STATION NIGHTLY

Waxen detritus waken:
devour red clay from the earth.
spindle arms held at one's side,
& gaunt.

        my tongue is polyanthean serpent,
        spitting venom upon every word
                            announced.

                                      April 10th, 2018

AGARTHA

Autumnal Dusk on Patoka Lake
for Cecilia

Ave, ave —
rustic Babylon,
faded to bristled Avalon:
the rock-throne
        crumbles,
crashing down,
beneath the weight —
        all water is glass.
mariners haven't spun
tales of
this shore, unforgiven,
engorged upon the finer cuisines
        cuisines of America —
America, amorous,
in which so many shout,
but softly, too.
America,
America —
shattered eyes
& hemorrhage,
    for the families,
      this strange city:
           October!
you've none for to
speak,
& Christmastime

hotel room —
back toward the North,
           far too soon.

ave, ave —
windowglass,
seaward,
Second Sun:
mere shadow cast
from behind cotton sky.
      "sea is milk,"
          someone
             spoke.
"20% not as much
      to sixpence Dickensian greed,
          & through the Aether" – shrugs –
   "better than nothing I reckon."
go off then.
flee!
    discover Andalusia
    & keep it hidden from me.
every mother,
a windowglass;
dark grey curtain,
drawn above the lapping surf.

sea, too, is glass
     as am I.

ave, ave —

AMONG THE STATUES THERE

jettison!
        in the high,
            both social & guilty
of that shouting
echoing on down
the beach;
rattle garbage cans
with your pinebox
rambling
& keep the neighbors up
        all night.
never met such a fellow
longing, prophetic, tied-off —
it is time to return
Upstate: green,
perhaps Eastern Coast…
should have heard the cackling
                branches, bare;
virgin lungs were
filled
with disease & exhaust.
        pondwater, also grey,
cannot light up my candle here
in the blended dark.
Korina
        & Avalon.
murky dreamland
of midtown scenery,
of those women,
& of substance between

        strangers
by nightfall —
but it is no longer,
for I have settled like a house
built upon two timber
                stilts
to keep the floodwaters
at the gate.
strangest blasphemies:
        "what if I found God?"
she asked
& the ground beneath her
sank.
ripple,
    grin,
        the hallway-light,
              picket-lines,
with Jamal on fire,
bathing Roman in the
city dusk/public square
    & crickets
are also grey
          …or had it been amphibious?
driftwood
driftwood
driftwood songs
& campground blues,
air is thin out here,
    with spindle locks.
geese heard,

never seen,
flying South, I suppose,
to the Gulf,
where the sea is glass
& plentiful —
            Gonsalves saw the sea's
windowglass, &
ghostly tile translucent
built the river up the ghostbroom,
& Benjamin saw
families on Mercury,
shrubbery saw variations of
fauna.
lifeguard   OFF DUTY,
        "stuff'll kill ya."
sharper aftertaste,
with glory
& brown spit,
brown against the dust:
that island where
no man
ventures,
save for the field mice —
I am such an island,
although I have not
woken up alone
in two mornings now.
seaglass is
also grey.
Tumbleweed,

bare scrub by winter,
sprawling wilderness
of the soul.

ave,
& chastity,
& acrimony —
feel desire
guiding one's face
to break the surface,
tobacco wad &
misted plain (invisible),
thievery,
   raucous
   ramblin',
gentrified the cityscape;
locals crushed
beneath the pressure,
cobweb-woven
   Lazarus.
those names, they
are bold,
hold up 'neath the voices
from the dining room,
like a sheet
caught in the rain —
it is heavy; hangs so heavily,
& Agartha: center of the Earth where
there is
  no
    pain,

AMONG THE STATUES THERE

nothing there to
fear.
& rumble forth,
jangling jester of
the horizon!
as fog on the
   14th
creeps upward
into the kitchen now,
my summertime has
since
passed me by —
   all hearts are also grey.
O Molly Moon!
she stands along the fence
in a spotlight
with her beer-scented wax
      ablaze,
I can nearly taste it.
Scraggle rocks wrought
steely daybreak far
below
& I remained unseen
through the centuries
there by the waterside.

whistlewind & liquor, too.
milk thistle & migraine
arrive in copious amounts of
squalor painted across
   the shoreline:

it is now that fabled American
sundown,
such a glowing endeavor
to be enacted here
within the misty bowels
    of the wood.
threadbare armies
tend to swoon & sway
along the dividing line
between evening & day
    — subjugate & congregate —
darlin' so lovely
in red,
in white,
& in blue, for to flood her
seafaring eye
strung along toward the
horizon-line.
cannot tempt fate,
cannot call upon
the one indebted
to stay.

O   bottlerocket blues!
O   jitterbug persuasion!
      Christ –
we are collectively
Pilate.
wooly denim
transfusion,

AMONG THE STATUES THERE

pray that the bluffs
do no crumble into
        the sea.
where have all
the nice girls gone? (a bloodshot conscience)
stripping the stowaway
of his right to choose
        "but, really, is it anyone's
        goddamn right?"
freedom – mere figure of speech
& of its bare application –
        any man's guess.

Loggy-Bottom:
that's what they said it meant,
uncertain as to
its origin,
while the old Saw-Man escaped
to that isle in days of pale
youth.
never came back.
    ave —
these folks have been so gracious
& kindly, unwilling to place
their interests before
   our own,
while farther on down the way,
Persephone is lost
from her cherubic romance
& Narmer is stranded from his

penicillin love —
3:21 this morning,
    coffee-tin kicks & glee,
rattled fools
& rattled obsolete,
ensnared by the thickets of ivy
grown beneath the surface —
whispers wet like
              black-market western jive
& faded evening clothes,
throat so raw -
    ave,
raw from steam,
    hurrah &
        ave!
all the cake & ice cream in eternity
could not ease
this affliction which has befallen them.
   colossal hallway, its congruency —
lampglown mist,
who will dissuade us at last from
    the Eastern Front?

finally –
they have placed
all the poets of the land
on trial &
the verdict was identical
   across the
           board:

AMONG THE STATUES THERE

solicitation & instigation
& embezzlement to
                    pandering
shanty, spectrum-class,
but not a one of those bastards,
with their corncob palaces
& lobbied cash,
are representative "of
       the laborious" —
     bunch of lousy
   fools to believe
   they are representative "of
       the laborious."

pack of Camels,
           nearly 8.00 a pop,
& they were trying
to drive us out
as we stood and cast   mortality blues in the dark:
      savages,
history in our eyes, with tin-pan recollections of
   the roses along the garden
                       wall
by clockwork &
late-arrival,
to plague thee.
clouds are also grey,
warring sea,
rocks are breakers:
       mossy kiss,

   bacterial flow,
cigarette butts
& ancient soda cans,
rusted to the bone,
stray within the crystal slipstream,
just as stale worry hanging
    in the empty cottage.
addendum &
adrenaline,
sterling cross,
cowboy/cobweb
& Corinthian with
cannons 'bout
the shore.
weed rustles,
pale moon shone &
mist drifts sheet-like
across the vacant land —
    so do it then,
cast me out!
with my Pacific
persuasion &
Byzantine grin,
sand & shells
are also grey &
upon fashion or
Fascism,
I could never truly
   rely,
while the homely &

AMONG THE STATUES THERE

the meek
grapple,
skimmed &
stoned,
ghostlike
grazing rooftops
with graceful baby-
        toes,
& tightened round bicep:
                        pumping
                  pumping
            pumping
       pumping

        "better this time around
            than before."

ocean-sprawl.
here is the North,
grand North,
where they were all so
emancipated or
incinerated,
    with their Romani feathers &
                      Martha's lies;
procession,
procession,
funeral marching bell
in procession;
distilled so deeply within

their musty casks of
              intention.
Rosanna.
misplaced specs
& seafloor
        tentacle:
the truest portrait of
the Ocean
we have ever
known —
& Rosanna,
       coral is also grey.
undertow
       (deathly & secretive
   & graceful &
           sublime),
innocent of any
wrongdoing
possibly committed
in lieu of women &
       sardonic humor:
that which is not
the name I carry.
all things now shall be
            vanquished!
                            "corn's gone; winter
                        must be coming."
wintertime,
wintertime,
brittle bone

AMONG THE STATUES THERE

& brittle
      cerebellum too,
asleep upon the
      carpeting
           for now,
never did mind it much at all
emerald & crystal
abound,
& Christian sensibility
has failed us, with its
nativity & contraband
weed tangled about
throughout   aqua;
fowls graze the surface,
worn
& wan.
destruction comes in
        waves,
slightest wave, frail
& icy beneath cascading
yellow leaves —
      October Eve,
      swashbuckling Horace,
so brazen 'neath beam
        of Ra.
concubine chemical
burns,
the lowly Adam in
   his garden (Jackson County ca. 1830),
& the gates are taken

by armies of the
                dreamt, now
contrivances,
haunting loathsome windows
& dusty storefronts
of   America
         America,
              where all has
                    fallen forth

                            upon those deafened
                                ears;
                            haunt missiles,
                            both, & gravity;
                            grey sea looks like
                            Salvo
                            in May:
                            extraterrestrial –
                            soft as Sunday noon,

something to ease
the frayed nerves within;
shadow-boxers on
the corner
making eyes at those
debutantes in the rain
across the way.

              & pray Guadalupe,
              finish your messiah.
kick the tin-can blues

AMONG THE STATUES THERE

which ail a generation,
propellers gnashing
   the mechanical surf —
      gazing,
           gazing Eye of Malta:
           great machinery purring &
                whirring out upon
           the water.

                                  October 12th, 2018

PART II

She's still with you, though harder to see these days, nearly a glass of gray lemonade in a twilit room…still she is there, cool and acid and sweet, waiting to be swallowed down to touch your deepest cells, to work among your saddest dreams.

— Thomas Pynchon,
Gravity's Rainbow

Hence every river, hence the spreading sea
And earth's pure bubbling fountains spring from thee.
— Orphic Hymn, "To Ocean"

PORTRAIT OF A LATE-AUGUST EVENING

Cicada tangled
                in the bedsheet, rigid shell
an emerald brooch:
                        8000 BCE the banks were settled,
                    by 5000, climate had
                            shifted —
      arthropod nestled softly in mud.
wounded
walnut trees
weep pale sunlight,
mourning the spirit
                within the statue   "ka," I believe was called,
while beneath humid (amethyst) – sometime after six o'clock –
      the oxen
           were much larger than the men,
                  only superior upon the register
                                then.

                                          August 28th, 2018

RECOLLECTIONS OF BATHING STREET AT NIGHT

Candlestick,
candle-moon —
songbird hums from within
cherry tree
— stroke of
twelve —
& velveteen fog obscures
the lovers' lamps.

smells like halite sea —
Gemini fever
through windowpane.
candle-moon —
final glow, night of
22nd

Water swills indigo
from the intersection
beside the culling-house.
tastes like stars
(the tidal wave, the
idle-windblown)
& rushes down the lane,
drowning bosom drowning light,
soft & misty descent.
pristine, the fog,

Austin C. Morgan

like virgin like waterflow,
hear it beneath & swills from
the grave; the dead
make love within the fog,
& the fields are drowned — all life
sprung by springtime overflown.

June 2019

HIGH MOON IN JULY

Late-night

The Winter may wash away ashen sin
onward toward our fairer equinox
and the pane of your morning's window mists
in faded defiance of meeker dawn.
the Sea shall turn to glass; the sky to sand
and roses bloom on windowsills so high —
the artistry of your face, a desert thus enchanted,
while within your song, such strange romantics;
your eyes, two elusive gems shone bright,
such dreams I long to know, to hold you close.
I shall love you in museum passages,
among the glow of gold and gleam of pearl.
now by the eveningfall, our eyes rest there,
with distance between our bedsides asleep
to never be apart within such dreams.

Disappointment

These lost gates of iron
give way to walls of sprawling ivy,
risen now into the haze of silver moon,
while revelry within accents the air
and ribbons of skeletal undergrowth
dance in nightly consequence there above.
I of little faith, I of timely farce,

lingering sleepily beyond and through
those walls of ivy, I am reborn now,
betrayed by the academics, betrayed
by the Proletariat (bastardry) —
sacred, dreamt letches 'neath the Common Sun.
I shall linger here against the shoreline
this profane fever I seek to ail – pride!

Kurt & Evelyn

There she lingers, from Ipanema to
The Benelux, like daffodils in sway
in springtime rain; "Sodade" is a song here.
lonesomeness at arm's length, he found her grown
as roses there, garden Melancholy,
long lost to history in springtime rain;
wind by crystal droplet, weather is fair –
all these dreams merely dreamt, unfurled in
her silken hair; "Sodade" is a song here.
every last setting sun, an omen, just
as each risen moon is a promise of
youth eternal in its shade, christened
and, thus, he prays to her in his finest
merchant's tongue: "come to me, find me up there.

January — August 2018

EASTERTIME BLUES

In Memory of Sam Shepard

I watched the crabapple beside the window:
coral was snow upon the grass
& roseate hung the heavy bough

— last time Dollface
   ever called up,
now he's wilting petals
   near the railroad track,
& in Montpelier, my eyes
had   closed & I heard
   summer whisper through
Ransom
      (my god it'd been so long) —
      all bungalows enchanted,
                   coral & juniper —
Coccinellidae
upon sleekest wind, across the spectral hour.

Scorpion!
harken to moon
   of your birth
& your moon
   is my moon
      (six vanished by Venus,
call her what you will)
   ravens-wing,
        citrine awash from
               Golden Hour prodigal dusk.

late-July
    (full on night of 27ᵗʰ)
& She (Columbia) led them Westward
across the great beersalt plain &
    ghostly desert beneath heavenly rock
& diamond hue, nightfall,
        till they reached the frothing sea blue by South &
                                  grey up
                                  above them,
although their finer bones were still
    stacked back at the Village Gate or had their shadows passed
    to Woodford as had he?

                cowboy see them off
                with their sashes of suede
                & musty cigarettes of a rainy
                afternoon

                Scorpion! see
                the moon
                of his birth
            & his moon
                is my moon,

    ravens-wing citrine
            awash by
                        Golden Hour prodigal dusk
    in late-July
            & Heaven too.

                                                July 2019

THE WITCHCAT

(Midsummer – Williams County, Ohio)

The Lovelands bloom tonight 'neath a
        tangy
                Hanna-Barbera dusk
  and the mist swells across
the edifice between —
by silver wind   the great Panther
           does glide,
eyes awash of Tuscany crisp,
        long, white as the stellae hung,
while beyond the old barndoor & a cabin's
windowglass, gazing
upon dim
           reflection across
           the glass (a gleaming
           face so far from the lamplit ease
           of home),
a familiar cast off into the heady
           twilight,
ruff, a blackened silhouette —
midnight
& by silver wind   the great Panther does

April 12th, 2018

SKETCHES FROM
THE CITY & THE SEA

Alone, watching the May moon above the trees
—William Carlos Williams

Alexandria

The reaching boughs of Christendom rattle, hollow-marrow and on high above the dusty passages etched into the earth where stalked savages and mathematicians alike, antlers forever locked in struggle to cleanse the icefield nightly, visitation and windowfront dancing of Neoplatonic prayer in awe of the laborer of the field, while sainted specters linger long in temple halls and the idols, golden, watch on with injustice and human travesty in their glare. The Glare. Captured within are young lovers and Beltane fathers, pagan figurines draped in white.

Ptolemy's tower brushing fingertips with communicants and their icons of green persuasion, the crowds gather about with cheers of joy, jeers of despair, echoing through dollhouse pillars of that which stood before. She, unseen, brows of coal and summer love. Mars, booming, cometh from skies of crimson, while Athena, of another school indeed, shields herself behind a plate of hay-yellow and how lovely she has become, to declare upon the cackling sea, the gurgling tide, birthing plasmid planets and animals of the spine for to creep upon the bare backs of daring lovers, youthful against the shore.

Her fate, since sealed, lingers high above as she walks with eyes cast forth — this teacher, this seer – soft as the day of May, russet glare sweeping city streets of billowing sand, to be executed in empire of the East, of the distance, a silhouetted realm against the cawing horizon line. As she moves, she moves as if to speak

>   those dreams of flowing water,
> flowing water trace an outline of love's face,
>   for whom I shall wait,
>   shall wait upon the passage
>   of
>   Time

    Ocean, calling aperture, empty cavern — time since lost to mortal men and wicked shadow, roars and spits upon the shore where they stand, commuters from the city of godly gain, to glance upon these sullen shores in their antiquity – Catharine! Roles reversed, as these are the shores of faunal saints, the groomsmen of pleasure.

    Beneath pale haze, twilight's citrine glow reveals our final star resting in the West. Wild boughs, tangled, blooming floral innocence, regained if only for a moment, and whispering toward the winds of days since passed. You have found striations of innocence there, and I have found you there, too.

The Dunes

Diana, they called her, upon catching glimpses of her nightly bath within the lake.

    Diana, keeper of the moonlight serenade, gray goddess waltzing bare skinned across the waves. In reality, her name had been something closer to grey and she had been fostered by students and intellectuals in Chicagoland; fluorescent tubing caught in flecks upon slick street-sides like shards of broken glass. They knew not her origins, nor her fate. Mythical, nearly, the fisherman spoke of her, lying in wait to view her nude and nightly lakefront cinema.

A genius – like Hypatia – her inquiries were placed among the stars which loomed like stage lightning to flicker and laugh high above the human thespian's dance. A box-step, forward and back, keeping time, never, ever lending.

Well you know that she settled in with a roughneck seaman, scuffled and grappled on tired the floor and crafted the damage to become her End. The poison had since filled her lungs before the course, that of the night in '25. Still a mystery, they have seen her splashing naked across the waves, seen her running through the trees by nightfall, never seeking forth the eyes. Oceanus, trickling in the dark. "Diana," they called her. "Diana of the Dunes."

Invisible Terraces (Troy)

Beneath the fields, cities buried.

Always, as in softly misted dream, we would find ourselves upon the crystal terraces of our city, La Luna, and you were often a lover, a dream of my own.

Hair, spindles strung of gold, lips pursed from sea to moon, and vain was she, the waves lapping her bare feet. In the sundown, I bowed my head and walked outside for to see, for to rest, for to breathe

> "Out among the cedars
> Sits an audience, demure.
> With an artist I fell away,
> And day by day, I chased her.
> Her father cast a vengeful eye,

I saw the lightening bright,
And as she fled, she began to bloom
Sullen petals of Byzantium,
Which scattered in her wake.
Up and down the winding coasts,
The city glossy upon awakening,
Shades of conceit,
We danced in fields,
We drank of wine,
But another with brownest eyes,
Never again would I find."

"Chicago"
For Kurt Cassidy-Gabhart

The great Lithuanian night crashes high above his head. His dear mother's words of laborer's heart flutter behind him as he passes through the grand American divide, divide upon with which one's days are filled with endless slaughter, racket of bones clanging nonchalantly upon higher shelves he is yet to reach. These corridors, a *jungle*, steel and mechanical belt coming down the line – hammer to this! hammer to that! – who carries the scythe?

ACTOR PORTRAYING (CLAD IN WORKMAN'S GARB): (thought, not spoken; glances upon the canvas): *This modernity – indecipherable to me,* (pushes up his cap and runs a hand through thick hair) *foolish dream of yours, boy.*

He is useless — a pretty-boy, if anything, and he plays his part with such bastardry, which he has borrowed from his own. Not that the old man had been absent, he was present, but maddened. His mother smoked cigarettes on the back porch where no one could find her. He, himself, had always been short on friends and frequent with gambling, sucking down that whiskey sour like snake bite venom in some deserted canyon.

CAMERAMAN: *Goddammit, it's cold out here!* He has already caught the flu – wan, icy-lipped and shivering, unsure as to whether his own internal tremors are a product of the low temperature or something more serious.

CUBIST: (Hemingway upon his breath – glides his fingers effortlessly across the intersecting lines, the language of features spoken upon a faceless specter) *See here, my good man — the nexus!*

But he sees not. The immigrant has but one thing on his mind – *sleep!* A few hours' sleep, then it's back to the factory.

ACTOR PORTRAYING: (tosses canvas to the concrete) *You waste my time with such banalities.*

— *film is spliced* —

retires to the field there upon the land his father owned. Better days. Better time for the muse, who stands, dress dancing in the breeze of summer evening. She is beautiful, for this is why he paints her.

DIRECTOR: *Just another moment, now hold still.*

His affluency with the brush being what had initially drawn her to his work. A naturalist to the fullest degree, the Director. For a moment, she is no longer the hired stand-in for the scene and the evening truly was that of summer without all of its machinery, that mechanical afternoon. For a moment she was his maiden, the nameless entity which he had viewed upon the stage. He gazed upon her, a gaze which she returned with a silent smile.

After its completion, the set was tidied by the crew and the Director shook hands, carried the folded script between the crook of his arm and shoulder.

[RL. VII] home in the darkness, he lights a cigar, as had the fevered cameraman prior, and hangs his coat before collapsing into the resting chair beside the window. In that moment, the desire for drink overtakes him, so he retreats from his resting chair and approaches the cabinet, pouring himself a whiskey, straight, and returns to his seat. As the liquid, laced ever-gently with the echo of roasted tobacco, burns his tongue and throat, he recalls her – not the actress, but the woman she had *portrayed* – of course, he couldn't give a damn about the actress…but what of that gaze, cast and met by one another, had she possibly resembled something for which he desires?

The night is long and lonesome, mired in blue shadow and the slightest hint of jazz seeps from just down the hall, and, like the immigrant, he shall return to work in a few hours, and, also like the immigrant, he shall be cursed to long with occasional lust and a constant swatch of melancholia shades to tint his waking days the episodic language of humanity: *nostalgia*.

Hitachi Province, Japan
Hollow ship, rosewood upon grey waves.

Vincennes

Well, it seems that the Kaiser has won your soul, wouldn't you say, Margreet?

Marguerite, title of such spawning beauty and gazing across the plain, hoping for some equation to tumble from space and line the walkways of her city in the rain.

AMONG THE STATUES THERE

    O Margarita! Doused all in satin, poised Venusian behind the rusting frame, your famed and lovely face of picturesque espionage. Sister Margaret shields our keen gaze from falling upon your ivory shoulders, just as the pastel glow emitted from that famed objet d'art is banished by rancorous hands to hide in antiquity behind stained glass of the keeper's hall. O Margarita! Hear my saintly city prayer!

    The cloak-and-dagger oligarchy placed so carefully behind the sun, the defendants of which carry a new falsehood upon each breath, it's crashing down as if the snow upon the firs had hardly even mattered. Hardly a patriot, no less a traitor, the cosmetic artist painted your eyes so many shades of blue, curled your hair as though you were the Madame in her garden, and lined you up against the wall — porcelain doll of Executioner's persuasion. You wore heels to crush the fallen shells in the aftermath of the smoke, the crashing thunder of allied guns – Margarita, beauty was the ultimate price to be paid.

(May — July 2018)

SONG OF TWO LOVERS
GLIMPSED FROM AFAR

What of this stranger
Eden
    I have found
        here in your
           arms?
mead moon, but a reflection
against the eye of the
    beholder —
such peculiar
    beauty,
force to reckoned with —
that saintly faunal melody, forestine beyond
the trees,
from which you had returned with
    baskets of
            wildflowers, satin boughs
            of the sprout,

  and petals
  for your   crown.

I present the gentile's
rivershell
   across the moon of
   my trembling palm,
& I'll ask of you please
     o please remain

Austin C. Morgan

(cut):
this marigold stem, its intuition
        of dust & foreign tongue,
                may the hand (right) strike
                in the moment of the Rose & say
      that you shall remain
      remain —
      & shall place a vacant kiss upon
      palest lips
            of my
                true love
                      once more.

                                (September 2018)

ON LOVE

(or carried softly & aglow within the crook of one's arm)

…& so Verlaine
once dreamt
velveteen
of the same strange
woman upon his stair,
night after night, curtain drawn by
        candlelight,
while Stendhal pined for
a lover, touch of whom
he would   never
               know,
& now in the valley green,
I have known the feeling
   well —
final crystalline salt drop of
this   vast
           & lachrymose sea, driftwood grey.

"lo son'
   la   luna"
         — (Old Ez in the medical tent)
& I am fragile
starglow,
shone high above as
        tattered remnants of
    pearl, pale as

Austin C. Morgan

    shards of broken
                    glass swept beyond the cloud —
so I am   defeated; I am ill-advised
in my attempt to beguile her,
        this woman beside
        the window.
well, she shall be made fresh by these
    tectonics in the early hours,
when the curtain has
been drawn by shadow, never cordial to
                    this candlelight.

September 2018

About the Author

Austin C. Morgan was born in Southern Indiana. He currently serves as a contributing editor to New York-based literary journal aaduna, Inc.

www.ingramcontent.com/pod-product-compliance
Lightning Source LLC
Chambersburg PA
CBHW020729100426
42735CB00038B/1103